SAINT P...

the Apostle

By REV. LAWRENCE G. LOVASIK, S.V.D.
Divine Word Missionary

NIHIL OBSTAT: Daniel V. Flynn, J.C.D., *Censor Librorum*
IMPRIMATUR: ✠ James P. Mahoney, D.D., *Vicar General, Archdiocese of New York*

SAUL IS PRESENT AT STEPHEN'S DEATH

AFTER the Holy Spirit came down on the Apostles and disciples, they were changed people. By their words and actions they drew many persons to Jesus.

To help in this work, the Apostles took on assistants. One of these was Stephen, who was filled with grace and wisdom and worked many signs among the people.

© 1980 by Catholic Book Publishing Corp., NY — Printed in Hong Kong

Some of the Jews grew to hate Stephen because he blamed them for failing to believe in the Son of God. A young man named Saul was one of them.

These men dragged Stephen outside the city and stoned him—even while he was praying for his murderers.

Stephen, filled with the Holy Spirit, looked to the sky above and saw the glory of God, and Jesus standing at God's right hand. "Look!" he exclaimed, "I see an opening in the sky, and the Son of Man standing at God's right hand."

As they stoned him Stephen prayed, "Lord, do not hold this sin against them." And with that he died.

Saul held the cloaks of the executioners and approved their act. He was a Pharisee from Tarsus and regarded Christians as preaching against the law of Moses. He thought he was right in persecuting them.

JESUS APPEARS TO SAUL

PAUL of Tarsus became the most bitter enemy that Christians had. He obtained letters from the high priest to take soldiers to Damascus and bring back Christians to Jerusalem in chains.

As Saul and his group drew near to Damascus, a great light shone around them. Saul looked up but fell to the earth blinded. He then heard a voice saying: "Saul, Saul, why do you persecute Me?"

"Who are You, Lord?" Saul asked. The voice answered: "I am Jesus, Whom you are persecuting."

Those that were with Saul saw the light, but they did not hear the voice. Saul then spoke: "Lord, what do You want me to do?"

The voice answered: "Arise and go into the city, and there you will be told what to do.

SAUL RECEIVES HIS SIGHT

WHEN Saul got up, he could not see. They led him by the hand into Damascus.

A disciple named Ananias was sent by God to Saul. He took him by the hand and said: "Brother Saul, receive your sight. God has chosen you to be His witness to all men."

Saul could now see again. He arose and was baptized in the faith of Jesus. He took the Greek Christian name of Paul.

PAUL ESCAPES IN A BASKET

PAUL and Ananias visited the Christians in Damascus. Paul preached to everyone that Jesus was the promised Savior and he offered proof of this from the Scriptures.

This angered the rulers of the people, who decided to attack Paul when he left the city.

But the Christians helped Paul escape. They put him in a basket and lowered it by means of a rope from a window above the city. So after three years Paul left Damascus.

BARNABAS SPEAKS FOR PAUL

P AUL went to Jerusalem and sought out the disciples of Jesus. But they remembered his former life and were afraid of him.

A disciple named Barnabas spoke for Paul to the Apostles and told what had happened. The Apostles then accepted him and he began working and preaching with them.

The Jews of Jerusalem hated Paul and tried to kill him. For his own safety, the Apostles sent him to the city of Tarsus in Asia Minor where he was born.

PAUL AND BARNABAS BEGIN THEIR JOURNEY

BARNABAS joined Paul in Tarsus and they went to one of the greatest cities of the Roman Empire—Antioch. They preached the Gospel there for one year.

The Spirit of God then directed them to go to the island of Cyprus, where the governor became a believer in Jesus. Later, they went to Asia Minor.

In every city, Paul preached first to the Jews and then to the Gentiles. He told them God was their Father and Jesus was their Savior.

Paul and Barnabas next traveled to a town called Iconium where a great crowd of Jews and Greeks accepted the faith. God proved the truth of their teaching by giving them the power to work miracles.

The two largest churches were the one in Jerusalem, of which James the cousin of Jesus was head, and the one in Antioch. But small churches were springing up everywhere, in all countries.

In this way the Gospel of Jesus became known among the pagans.

THE CURE OF THE LAME MAN

PAUL and Barnabas came to the city of Lystra, where there was a man lame from birth. When Paul saw him, he called out in a loud voice: "Stand up on your feet!"

At once the man leaped up and walked, praising God. He followed the two Apostles before all the people who looked upon them as gods and wanted to worship them.

The Apostles urged the people to turn away from evil and pray to the one true God.

PAUL IS STONED

WITHIN a few days, some Jews stirred up the people against Paul and Barnabas. The mob threw stones at Paul. Thinking he was dead, they dragged him outside the city.

But the Christians came to Paul and took care of his wounds. They were glad that he was able to speak once more.

Barnabas had not been stoned. So he took Paul to another city—Antioch in Syria.

PAUL PREACHES THE END OF SACRIFICES

LONG before the coming of Jesus, the Jews had offered up animals in sacrifice to the Lord. Some converted Jews argued that Christians still had to obey the law and sacrifice animals.

Paul and Barnabas disagreed. They all went back to Jerusalem to meet with the Apostles and to settle the matter.

The Holy Spirit informed them that animal sacrifice was no longer necessary. The Lord wanted His people to obey the words of the Gospel and believe in His Son Jesus.

THE GIRL WITH THE EVIL SPIRIT

PAUL now took Silas and went to Syria. At Lystra they met Timothy who became a believer and went with them to Philippi in Macedonia.

They saw a poor slave girl who told fortunes for money through the power of an evil spirit. Paul cured her and she could no longer tell fortunes.

Her master, who used to take all the money, was very angry. Out of revenge, he had Paul and Barnabas dragged to the market place and brought before a judge.

PAUL AND SILAS IN PRISON

PAUL and Silas were whipped and thrown into prison. Their feet were locked in stocks, heavy pieces of wood with two holes in the middle just large enough to encircle an ankle.

At midnight while Paul and Silas were praying, the prison doors were torn away by an earthquake and the stocks of the prisoners were opened.

But no prisoners left. Paul preached to them and the jailor. Before morning every one of them was baptized.

PAUL IN ATHENS

PAUL and Silas were released from prison for both were Roman citizens. Their whipping and imprisonment had been against the law.

They preached in other cities of Greece until they came to Athens, the most important city. It was famous for wisdom but its people worshiped idols.

Paul spoke in the highest court about the true God and His only Son Who had risen. Many laughed but some believed.

PAUL IN CORINTH

PAUL traveled to Corinth where he preached in the synagogue and in the house of a man named Justus.

Paul wrote two letters to the churches at Thessalonica, encouraging them in their faith. He stayed there for eighteen months and supported himself by his trade as a tentmaker.

One night he had a vision and heard the voice of God telling him not to be afraid, for He had many friends in that city. And indeed many people in Corinth became believers.

PAUL IN EPHESUS

PAUL next went to the city of Ephesus where he worked for three years and converted many people to Christianity. The believers gave up worshiping the goddess Diana.

Therefore, many Ephesians no longer bought tiny statues of Diana made of brass and silver by skilled workmen.

One of these workers was angered at losing business and aroused the crowd against Paul. But the Apostle moved on to Macedonia, preaching in one city after another.

PAUL IN JERUSALEM

PAUL'S enemies were strongest in Jerusalem. But his great love for Jesus drove him to return there. The Christians greeted him with joy.

Paul spoke out boldly to the crowds of Jews about Jesus. Some of his enemies seized him and cried out. "Men of Israel, help! This man speaks against the people, the law, and the Temple.

They dragged Paul outside the Temple and shouted: "Away with him."

PAUL ADDRESSES THE JEWS

THE captain of the Roman soldiers rescued Paul from the angry mob. Paul spoke to the people but again they became angry because he mentioned the Gospel, and tried to kill him.

He was put in prison for his own safety. The next day he again spoke to the great Council of Jews. Once more there was an uproar.

The soldiers had to bring Paul back into prison because the people would have killed him.

PAUL'S VISION

THE following night Paul had a vision. The Lord stood beside him and said: "Be of good cheer, Paul, for as you have testified of Me in Jerusalem, so must you bear witness in Rome."

Meanwhile his enemies planned to kill Paul when he was sent to the council. Paul learned of this and told the Roman captain.

So the captain sent Paul to the Roman governor of Judea, who was called Felix and lived at Caesarea.

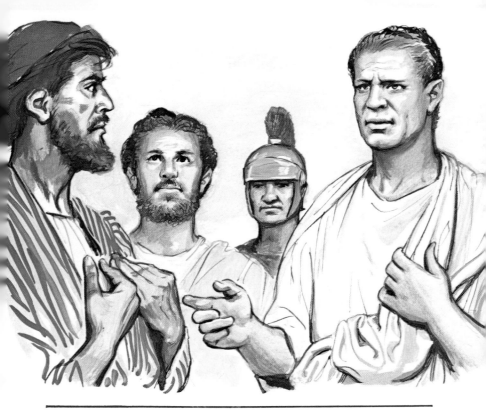

PAUL IN CAESAREA

FELIX listened to Paul defend himself and found him guilty of nothing. He jailed Paul but gave him much freedom—even letting him come to his own house to speak with him.

After two years, Festus became governor. He wanted to send Paul to Jerusalem but Paul knew he would be killed there. So he asked to go to the court of Caesar at Rome.

As a Roman citizen, Paul had this right.

PAUL'S DEFENSE BEFORE KING AGRIPPA

KING Agrippa and his wife, Bernice, came to Caesarea to visit the new governor. Festus told him about Paul.

Agrippa listened to Paul and exclaimed: "Paul, you almost persuade me to be a Christian!"

The King and the governor concluded that Paul did not deserve death or prison. He would be freed if he had not appealed to the Roman court.

THE STORM AT SEA

PAUL was put on a ship with other prisoners and sent to Rome in the care of soldiers. Luke and another friend went along to care for the aging Apostle.

A heavy storm arose and continued for many days. The ship was in danger of sinking.

Paul calmed the men by assuring them that God would not let anyone die, although the ship would be destroyed. He then took bread, thanked God for it, and began to eat. The soldiers also ate and felt more cheerful.

PAUL
SHIPWRECKED

IN all there were 276 people on the ship. While trying to reach the shore for safety, the ship ran aground. It began to break up under the wild waves of the sea.

Because of Paul, the soldiers did not kill the prisoners to keep them from escaping. Those who could swim were told to jump into the sea and get to shore. The rest floated in on boards and broken bits of the ship itself. Every one of the people arrived safely on land.

PAUL HEALS THE SICK

THE voyagers learned that they had arrived at an island called Malta. A poisonous snake fastened itself on Paul's hand but he shook it into the fire. And it did him no harm.

The islanders were astonished at this and became kind and friendly. Paul healed all the sick through the power of the Holy Spirit.

They stayed on this island most of the winter, and when a ship left the harbor they continued their journey to Rome.

PAUL IN ROME

AT last, the prisoners, including Paul, reached Rome safely. Paul spent two years there. He was allowed to live in his own house, with a soldier to watch him.

Paul taught everyone who came to him about Jesus. Many believed and no one tried to prevent Paul from preaching.

Paul welcomed every person who came to his house to be taught—Jew or Gentile.

PAUL VISITS OTHER COUNTRIES

AT the end of the year 62, Paul was set free from his "house arrest" and continued his missionary journeys.

He probably traveled to Spain and then visited Crete and left Titus in charge of the Church there.

Paul also returned to Ephesus and placed Timothy at the head of the Church there. He went on to Troas where he left his cloak and his books to a man called Carpus.

Finally, Paul passed on to Nicopolis where he spent the winter. Although he was 60 years old, he never stopped laboring for Christ.

Paul once wrote to the Christians: "My brothers, we beg and exhort you in the Lord Jesus that, even as you learned from us how to conduct yourselves in a way pleasing to God, so you must learn to make still greater progress.

"You know the instructions we gave you in the Lord Jesus. It is God's will that you grow in holiness. God has called us to holiness."

PAUL IS IMPRISONED ONCE AGAIN

PAUL once wrote these beautiful words to the Romans: "Who will separate us from the love of Christ? Trial, or distress, or persecution, or hunger, or nakedness, or danger, or the sword? Yet in all this we are more than conquerors because of Him Who has loved us.

"For I am certain that neither death nor life will be able to separate us from the love of God that comes to us in Christ Jesus, our Lord."

And it was by the sword that Paul gave his life for the love of God and Jesus Christ, His Son. In the year 66, he was arrested a second time and sent to Rome as a captive.

The Emperor Nero blamed the Christians for burning the city of Rome. The people rose up in anger against the Christians and put thousands of them to death.

Surrounded by his closest friends, Timothy, Luke and Mark, Paul was brought to trial again. This time he was condemned to death.

Paul wrote: "I am being offered as a sacrifice. The time of my death is near. I have fought the good fight, I have finished the race, I have kept the faith. From now on a merited crown awaits me; on that Day the Lord, just judge that He is, will award it to me—and not only to me but to all who have looked for His appearing with eager longing."

PAUL — THE HERO OF FAITH

THERE has never been a greater preacher and missionary than Paul. He spent his life telling people about Jesus. He founded churches all over Asia Minor and Greece.

Paul wrote many letters to the churches he had founded, explaining about Jesus. They became parts of the New Testament. The Spirit of God helped him, telling him what to write, so his letters are God's word.

Paul was a great hero. He suffered very much for his beloved Master. Five times he was cruelly beaten. Once he was stoned and left for dead. Three times he was shipwrecked, and once he was in the water a whole day and a night, kept afloat only by some piece of a ship.

But many beautiful things happened to Paul, too, which strengthened him for his work. Jesus spoke to him right out of heaven, as Paul was going to Damascus. Many times God spoke to him, bringing comfort and hope.

Once in a vision Paul saw the glories of heaven and heard words so wonderful that no man could ever speak them.

We should try to imitate St. Paul in his love for Jesus and His Church. We should pray to him for all the missionaries who are continuing his work throughout the world.

PAUL — CHRIST'S MARTYR

AFTER thirty years of untiring labor, long travels and constant persecution, Paul the great Apostle of Jesus Christ, finally died the death of a martyr. He was beheaded about the year 67 in Rome.

The Church honors Paul on two feast days: The Feast of Saints Peter and Paul (June 29) and The Conversion of Saint Paul (January 25).